By Jim Drewett

CONTENTS

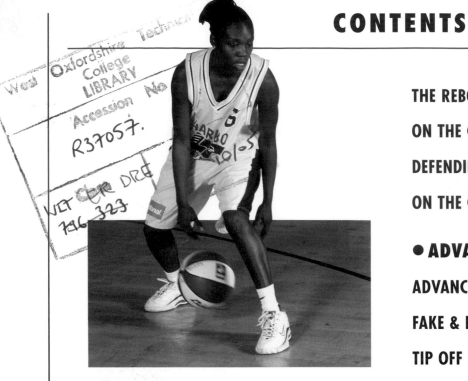

£ 3.99

INTRODUCTION

Lightning quick and loaded with skill, basketball is one of the world's most popular games. Its colour, razzmatazz and million dollar superstars make it a fantastic spectator sport, and millions of people tune into games in America's NBA league every week. But it is a great game to play too, and we want this book to inspire you to get out there and shoot some hoops!

GUIDE TO SYMBOLS & ARROWS

Throughout this book you will find helpful illustrations to show you how to do a drill. Unless specified, the lines and arrows are used to represent the following.

To help you understand the terms in this book, we have used the following...

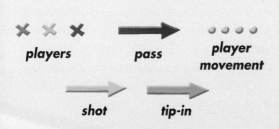

players pass player movement

shot tip-in

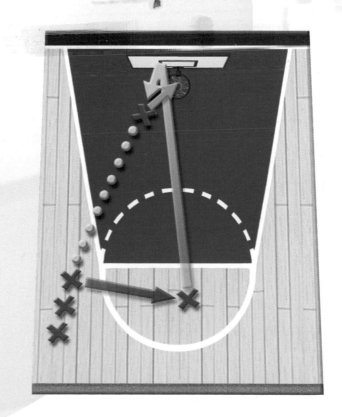

THE COURT

Basketball may be one of the world's most popular games, but it is also one of the most simple. The court shown here is for a proper match, but all you really need for a great game of basketball is a ball, a basket and a smooth floor.

THE COURT

A pro basketball court is 28.5 metres (94 ft) long and 15 metres (50 ft) wide. The best courts have polished wooden flooring, although any smooth surface will do.

THE BASKET & BACKBOARD

At each end of the court is the basket, which overhangs the end-line. The hoop is set at 3.05 metres (10 ft) from the ground. Behind the hoop is a backboard that is 1.8 x 1.05 metres (6 ft x 3½ ft), off which the ball may rebound. On pro courts this board is usually see-through so it doesn't obstruct the view of spectators.

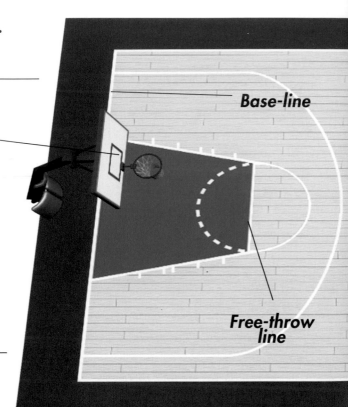

Base-line

Free-throw line

TEAMS

Basketball teams can have anything from between ten to twelve players, but only five are allowed on the court at any one time. The coach decides which five he wants on the court, and he can bring players on and off (when there is a break in play) all through the game.

THE BASICS

To move the ball, players can pass to a team-mate, or dribble. Dribbling means bouncing the ball along the ground while walking or running.

SCORING

The object of basketball is to score more points than the opposition. To score points, teams must score baskets – in other words shoot the ball through their own hoop. Where they score from determines how many points they score.

RESTRICTED AREA

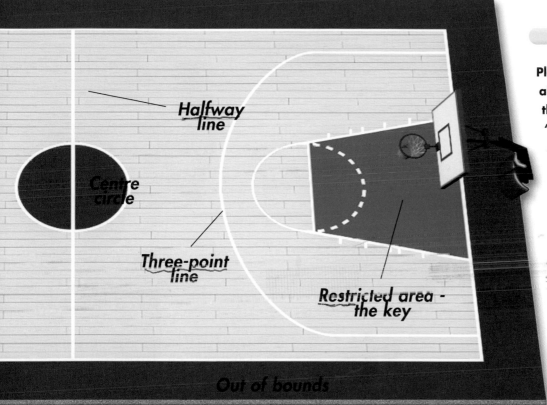

Players are only allowed to step inside their opponents' 'key' for three seconds at a time (the areas coloured blue in this diagram).

Halfway line

Centre circle

Three-point line

Restricted area – the key

Out of bounds

POINTS

3 points
A basket scored from anywhere outside the three-point line (also known as a field goal).

2 points
A basket scored from anywhere inside the three-point line.

1 point
A basket scored from a free-throw line when a free throw is awarded after a foul.

*W*ith basketball fashion becoming almost as big as the sport itself, make sure that you choose your kit because it is practical and comfortable, not because of how it looks!

TRACKSUIT

Because basketball players spend a lot of time sitting on the bench, it is important that they have a tracksuit to keep themselves warm when they are not in the thick of the action. The tracksuit trousers should be loose fitting, or at least have zips at the bottom so that they can be removed quickly when a player is called off the bench.

THE BALL

A full-sized basketball is made from leather, rubber or a synthetic material. It has a circumference of between 75–78 cm (29–31 inches) and must be blown up to weigh between 567–650 g (20–22 oz).

SHOES

The most important piece of kit is the footwear. With so much running, jumping, twisting and turning in basketball, it is crucial to make sure that you have the right kind of shoes. Usually made from a combination of leather and plastic, there are two main types of basketball shoe to choose from:

LOW TOPS:

Some players find lower cut basketball shoes more comfortable, although these still offer a fair amount of support around the ankle.

Notice how strong the upper part of the shoe is, offering protection to the feet in the rough and tumble of a crowded basketball court.

VEST

A basketball vest should be light and loose-fitting. It is important that the movement of the shoulders and arms is not impaired, which is why it is sleeveless. The vest should also feature tiny air holes to keep the body cool.

PRACTISE HOOP

It is great for players to get a practise hoop set up at home or at school. The best kind can simply be fixed to a wall, with the hoop 3.05 metres (10 ft) above the ground. The practise hoop should be set up where the ground is smooth (ideally concrete or tarmac) and away from any doors and windows.

SHORTS

Again, these should be light and comfortable, and big enough to allow complete freedom of movement.

SOCKS

Socks are surprisingly important in basketball, as players' feet take such a pounding. They should be soft and relatively thick to prevent blisters.

HIGH TOPS:

High top basketball boots give the ankles strong support, which basketball players need.

The upper part of the boot is tough and durable, but also soft, comfortable and very, very light.

SOLES:

Modern basketball shoes have air-cushioned soles to protect the ankles and soles of the feet when players land heavily after high jumps.

The soles are made from rubber, offering high grip on the court surface.

DRIBBLING

You are not allowed to walk or run while holding the ball in basketball, which makes dribbling one of the first skills to be mastered. It is not only important to keep the ball under control and away from opponents, but also to do it at speed.

BASIC DRIBBLING

While you are dribbling, at least one foot must stay in contact with the ground and you can only use one hand at a time. And remember, once you have stopped with the ball you must pass or shoot; you cannot start dribbling again.

STEP 1
Do not look at the ball, keep your head up so that you can see the other players on the court.

STEP 2
Using your fingers and your wrist, push the ball downwards and slightly ahead of you with a clean, smooth action.

STEP 3
Allow your fingers and wrist to move smoothly up and down with the ball. Do not let the ball make contact with the palm of your hand, feel it with your fingers and shift it with your wrist.

STEP 4
As you move forwards, bend your knees and keep your body over the ball to shield it from opponents. Always dribble with the hand that is farthest away from your opponent.

When there is an opponent in your way, you can beat him by stopping, changing hands and dribbling away in the opposite direction.

STEP 1

As you dribble across your opponent, stop suddenly on the foot nearest him. Remember to keep the ball away from your marker.

STEP 2

Turn your body back the other way, pivoting (see page 12) on the foot nearest the marker. Keep your back turned to him to shield the ball.

STEP 3

Keep turning until you are facing the opposite direction. As you bounce the ball at the end of your turn, collect it with your other hand (now farthest from your marker) and continue play.

TOP TIP

The reverse dribbling technique must be executed in one quick, smooth motion to outfox your opponent.

ON THE COURT: DRIBBLING

Practise your dribbling with these simple drills, designed to improve your ball control.

DRIBBLING REACTION (2–6) PLAYERS

This drill is great for helping you to learn the most important rule of dribbling; look forward and not at the ball.

STEP 1

Players dribble the ball in a standing position, looking forward at a coach or another player standing a few metres ahead.

STEP 2

When the coach or other player raises his arm, the players stop dribbling, that way the players must be looking at him to know when to stop.

PROGRESSION

Instead of dribbling from a standing position, walk and then run with the ball towards the coach.

DRIBBLING CONES (1–10) PLAYERS

In a match situation you will not be dribbling in a straight line very often!

Set up a line of cones, placing them about 0.5 metres (2 ft) apart. Then simply dribble in and out of them using one hand. Start off slowly, then speed up. As you improve, try switching hands. You will find this makes dribbling through the cones easier.

DRIBBLING TAG (2–10) PLAYERS

This drill teaches you to protect the ball while you dribble.

Simply mark out an area just big enough to contain the number of players. Each player has a basketball which they must dribble continuously. While dribbling and protecting their own ball, they must also try to knock the opponents' balls out of their hands. When a player loses their ball or stops dribbling they must leave the area. The winner is the last player left dribbling the ball.

TRAFFIC JAM DRIBBLING (3–15) PLAYERS

This drill is good for all dribbling techniques, because it requires you to keep your head up, change hands and speeds, and protect the ball all at the same time.

STEP 1

Three or more players (each with a basketball) stand in a circle, ideally around the centre circle. Players must dribble in a straight line to the other side of the circle, all starting at the same time.

STEP 2

Then they will all converge in the middle as they pass through the centre of the circle.

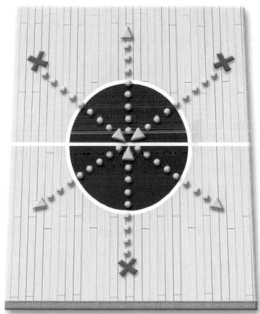

STEP 3

Only by cleverly dribbling the ball through this 'heavy traffic' will they make it to the other side.

TOP TIP

If you have enough players, make the circle two or three deep so that when the first players have made it through, they can pass the ball to the next set of players and go to the back of the line to wait for another turn.

BALL HANDLING

Basketball is so quick, it is crucial that as soon as you get the ball you get it under control and keep it well protected from the opposition.

CATCHING GRIP

This is the grip favoured by pro basketball players. Place your non-shooting hand on the side of the ball, gripping with your fingers, while your shooting hand is positioned behind the ball, with your palm facing forwards. This makes either passing or shooting an easy option.

shooting hand

TRIPLE THREAT POSITION

The triple threat position is the basic body position that you should adopt on receiving the ball. Standing with your legs apart, holding the ball firmly into your chest (keeping your body between the ball and your opponent) will give you time to decide your next move.

PIVOTING

When you stop with the ball, you are allowed to change direction – as long as you do not move the foot on which you stopped. This is called pivoting, and you may want to use it to turn and 'square up' to the basket.

STEP 2
Lift your non-pivot foot up and begin to turn your body round, using short steps for balance.

STEP 3
Keep your knees bent, your back straight and your head up. When you complete the pivot, you should end up in the triple threat position again.

STEP 1
Once you have decided to turn, lift the heel of your pivot foot up and shift your bodyweight over it.

When you catch the ball in mid-air, you are allowed to take a step to stop. Using the stride stop allows you to stop legally, and it can also be used at the end of a dribble.

STEP 1
Move towards the pass, stretching your hands out and keeping your eyes on the incoming ball.

STEP 2
As you catch it, step forward with your leading foot. This becomes your pivot foot and counts as a step.

STEP 3
Bring yourself to a halt with your second step. You should end up in a balanced triple threat position with your head up and your knees bent, leaving you ready to pass or shoot.

The beauty of the jump stop is that it only counts as one step, so you can choose either foot as your pivot foot.

STEP 1
Jump towards the ball with both feet parallel.

STEP 2
Catch the ball in mid-air, then make sure that you land with both feet touching the ground at the same time.

TOP TIP
After completing a jump stop, and once you have pivoted on one foot, you cannot switch to the other.

PASSING

The easiest way for a basketball team to keep possession of the ball is by passing it, and it is also a much quicker way to move the ball up the court than dribbling. There are three main types of pass to choose from, depending on the game situation, your position on the court and that of your team-mates and opponents.

CHEST PASS

The chest pass is the safest and most accurate pass in basketball, but it can only be made when you have a clear path between yourself and the pass receiver.

STEP 1
Hold the ball to your chest with both hands. Your thumbs should be behind it and your fingers either side.

STEP 2
Grip the ball firmly and flex your wrists backwards. Step forwards and extend your arms sharply in the direction of the receiver.

STEP 3
As your arms straighten, release the ball firmly with a flick of the wrists. Your fingers should be pointing in the direction you want the ball to go, with your thumbs downwards.

TOP TIP
Don't watch the ball as you make the pass –
keep your eyes on your intended target.

If you can't pass directly to a team-mate because there is an opponent in the way, you may have to go over him or her. To do this, use the overhead pass.

STEP 1

Hold the ball above your head with your fingers cupping the underside of the ball, keeping it out of reach of your marker.

STEP 2

Release the ball just above your head, using a short, sharp flick of the wrists and a short forward movement of the arms. Make sure your eyes are on the intended target.

Another way to pass when you are tightly marked is with the bounce pass.

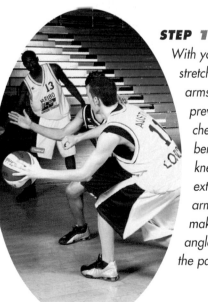

STEP 1

With your marker stretching his arms out to prevent the chest pass, bend your knees and extend your arm out to make the angle for the pass.

STEP 2

Bounce the ball to your team-mate. Because the ball will slow down when it hits the floor, aim for the ball to hit the floor about two-thirds of the way to the receiver – this will reduce the chance of an interception.

ON THE COURT: PASSING

Become a pass master with the help of these great passing exercises and drills.

WALL PASSING (1 PERSON)

STEP 2

As the ball bounces back off the wall, catch it and repeat. Try to vary the passes, using a combination of chest, overhead and bounce passes.

STEP 1

Simply stand a few yards from the wall, and throw the ball against it. Imagine that you are passing the ball through the wall to someone opposite you.

As you improve your passing and ball-handling skills, you will get used to dealing with powerful, difficult passes and moving the ball on quickly.

PIGGY IN THE MIDDLE (3 PLAYERS)

This is a classic drill; great for sharpening up those passing skills. It is good for working on 'piggy's' defensive play too.

STEP 1

Two players stand about 3.5 metres (10 ft) apart. They must pass the ball to each other, while a third (defensive) player stands between them and tries to block or intercept the ball.

STEP 2

When the player in the middle has touched the ball once, swap positions with a passing player.

TOP TIP

The passing players should not use overhead passes as it makes it too easy to by-pass the 'piggy'.

This is a great drill for improving your passing and catching – under pressure.

TWO-PLAYER PASSING DRILL

STEP 1

Two players line up opposite each other, about 3.5 metres (10 ft) apart, both with basketballs in their hands. On the call of three, each player must pass the ball to the player opposite.

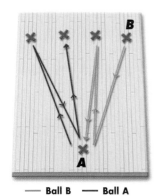

STEP 2

One player must play a chest pass while the other plays a bounce pass . As soon as the players catch the ball, they should pass it back immediately, maintaining a constant, fast-moving drill.

Build up speed gradually to improve your reaction time.

MACHINE GUN PASSING (5 PLAYERS)

In a game of basketball the action comes thick and fast, which is why this lightning-quick passing drill is so useful.

— Ball B   — Ball A

STEP 1

Stand four players in a semi-circle, all facing a fifth player (player A) who stands about 2.5 metres (8 ft) away. Player A has a basketball in his hands, as does one of the players in the semi-circle, player B.

STEP 2

After the whistle, player A passes the ball quickly to one of the players in the semi-circle, calling out the name of the intended receiver. As soon as the ball has been released, player B quickly passes his ball to player A. Player A receives it, then passes it to another player in the semi-circle. This cycle continues in quick, rapid-fire succession requiring good reactions and concentration.

Each player should call the name of the intended receiver when passing.

SHOOTING

*A*nyone in a team can score a goal, so perfecting your shooting
techniques is vital for scoring points.

THE SET SHOT

**The set shot is used when you are standing still, relatively close to
the basket. It is also the kind of shot you would use for a free throw.**

STEP 1

*From a standing position with
your knees slightly apart, crouch
down facing the basket. If you
are shooting with your right
hand, your right leg should
be slightly further
forward than your left.*

STEP 2

*With your non-shooting hand gripping the side of the ball
and your shooting hand facing towards the basket, begin to
straighten your legs and spring up towards the basket.*

STEP 3

*Lift yourself up on to your toes
in one movement. Use your
non-shooting hand to steady
the ball, then shoot with a
strong flick of the wrist.*

THE JUMP SHOT

**Often the only way to get your shot past an
opponent in front of you is to jump and
release the ball in mid-air.**

STEP 1

*With your feet flat on the floor
facing the basket, crouch down
low to give you enough force to
jump off the ground.*

STEP 2

*Straighten up, bringing the ball
into the shooting position as you
rise with the elbow of your shooting
arm directly beneath the ball.*

STEP 3

*Spring off the ground to shoot above
the reach of any defender. Focus on
the basket as you release the ball.*

Unlike the previous two shots, the lay-up is used when you are on the move. It is all about driving right to the basket and using the backboard to help you score.

STEP 1

Approach the basket from the side as you dribble towards it. Put all your weight on your front leg – if you are right-handed then this should be your left leg – and bend your knee to give you the spring to jump.

STEP 2

Spring off your forward leg, raising your arms ready to throw the ball.

Your action should be one continuous and smooth movement, and you should keep your eyes on the basket at all times.

STEP 3

Jump up towards the basket (go up to the side of it, not directly in front of the hoop). As you reach the top of your jump, transfer the ball to your shooting hand, extend your arm as far as it will go and release the ball.

STEP 4

The ball should bounce off the backboard and go softly into the hoop.

TOP TIP

Aim for the small rectangle on the backboard. The perfect shot should hit the top corner of the rectangle, on your side of the basket.

ON THE COURT: SHOOTING

It is crucial that when you get a shooting chance in a basketball match you make it count, because if you miss, your team may well lose the ball. That is why – even for top players – it is crucial to practise shooting.

ONE-PLAYER DRILL

Stand close to the basket and practise set shots and jump shots from the same point.

Keep shooting until you can get five of each in a row, then move to another spot. Move farther out from the basket or change your angle. Try shooting with both hands, too.

Every time you shoot, picture the ball going into the basket. If you believe you are going to score, you probably will.

AROUND THE WORLD (1-2 PLAYERS

This drill teaches you to vary your shooting distance and angle around the basket.

Stand on one of the marks on the key closest to the basket and shoot. If you score, fetch the ball and move onto the next mark. If you miss, remain on your spot until the next go. See how quickly you can go around the key from 1 to 10, scoring baskets (including the free-throw line and a field goal position on the outside of the key). Set a record, then try to beat it!

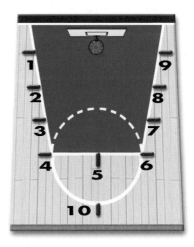

TOP TIP

Try racing a friend. This added pressure teaches you to get into position and shoot quickly, just as you would have to do in a match situation.

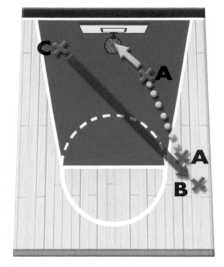

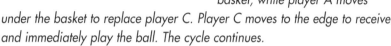

Keep things moving with this lay-up shooting drill, which also provides rebounding and passing practise.

Two players (A and B) stand on the edge of the key to the right of the basket, while a third (player C) stands just to the left of the basket. Player A approaches the basket and attempts a lay-up shot. Player C collects the ball and passes it back to player B at the edge of the key. Player B now runs at the basket, while player A moves under the basket to replace player C. Player C moves to the edge to receive and immediately play the ball. The cycle continues.

This is another fast-moving drill involving three players – two providers and one shooter. It allows the shooter to get into a good rhythm.

Try to increase the speed of passing and shooting to build up the rhythm.

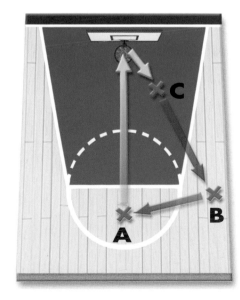

The shooter (player A) stands on the edge of the key. Player B stands on the other side of the key and player C waits under the basket. Player A shoots, player C collects the ball and passes it quickly to player B. Player B passes it swiftly on to player A who shoots again. When player A has five attempts, all the players move round one position and the drill starts again.

THE REBOUND

When someone takes a shot, there's a good chance that it will bounce off the backboard or the hoop. This is called a rebound, and winning the ball from this situation is a crucial part of the game.

BOXING OUT

When a player shoots, you must attempt to put yourself between the basket and your opponent. This is called boxing out, and is used to win the rebound.

STEP 1

As the shot is made, anticipate a rebound by positioning your body between the hoop and your marker.

STEP 2

Watching the ball at all times, bend your knees and spread out your arms, making your body big and strong. Get ready to jump up as it rebounds.

TIPPING-IN

If you are on the attack near the hoop and you judge the rebound perfectly, rather than catching the ball and then having a shot you can try to tip the ball straight back into the basket without landing. Be warned, though, this is tough!

Tipping-in is a very difficult skill to perfect, and requires good judgement and a spectacular jump. As you watch the flight of the shot, anticipate the rebound and launch yourself into the air just as the ball hits the rim or the backboard. Adjust your body in mid-air and try to get a hand to it. If you can get there, try to guide the ball into the basket with a gentle flick of the hand.

TOP TIP

The secret of tipping-in is to guide the ball into the basket, not shoot it in. Usually it will only require the lightest of touches to guide the bouncing ball back into the basket.

As a defender, if you catch a rebound from an opposition shot, you regain possession for your team, which turns your defence instantly into an attack.

STEP 1

By boxing out your opponent, you have made yourself favourite to win the ball if it rebounds. When it does, aim to catch it at the highest point possible. Doing this is all about timing your jump. Don't jump too early or you may find yourself on the way down as the ball reaches catching height.

STEP 2

As you catch the ball, turn away from your nearest opponent so that the ball is shielded as you land.

It is just as crucial for attacking players to follow up on rebounds as it is for defenders. Regaining control of the ball means the attack stays alive and you or your team may still score.

Just like defensive catching, the secret to successful offensive rebound play is position, anticipation and timing. Try to outfox the defensive marker who is trying to block you by faking to move one way then darting the other. Try and get yourself into the boxing out position so that you are better placed to time your jump and win the ball. If you win the ball and have enough space, jump straight back up and shoot!

ON THE COURT: REBOUNDING

It may be more fun to practise shooting and dribbling, but rebounding is so crucial to the game of basketball that it is important to find time to sharpen up your play.

ONE-PLAYER DRILL

When your have perfected your catching, practise shooting as soon as you have landed, or pivoting back towards the opposite end of the court as if you were defending.

STEP 1

Stand under the basket, 1.5 metres (5 ft) away from the base-line, and shoot the ball against the backboard.

STEP 2

As the ball rebounds, jump and catch it. Work on timing your leap so that you jump forward to meet the ball, catching it at the highest point you can.

TIPPING-IN DRILL (2-10 PLAYERS)

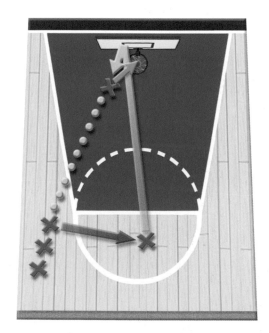

A line of players, each with a ball, stands outside the key, to one side of the free-throw line. One by one they pass their ball to a player standing on the free-throw line who shoots at the backboard so that the ball rebounds. The player who has passed the ball follows up on the shot, jumps and tries to tip the ball directly in. Then he collects his ball and goes to the back of the line while the next player begins the routine. If the rebound cannot be tipped-in, catch it and shoot.

Two opposing players (A and B) stand in the centre of the key, 1.8 metres (6 ft) away from the basket. While they try to block each other out, a third player (C) shoots at the backboard from the free-throw line. Players A and B must compete to catch the rebound. Adjust the drill by making A an attacking player and B defensive. While A must try to tip-in or shoot from the rebound, B must try to catch the ball or block A's attempts at scoring. For a further progression add two more players, one attacking and one defending, to re-create a match-type rebound situation.

PROGRESSION 1

Adjust the drill by making A an attacking player and B defensive. While A must try to tip-in or shoot from the rebound, B must try to catch the ball or block A's attempts at scoring.

PROGRESSION 2

For a further progression add two more players, one attacking and one defending, to recreate a match-type rebound situation.

ONE-ON-ONE REBOUND DRILL (3 PLAYERS)

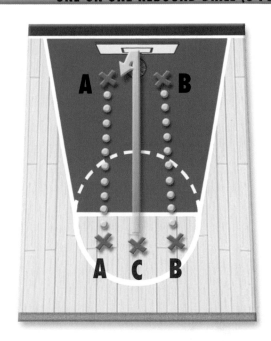

DEFENDING

Just as every player on a basketball team must be able to pass and shoot, every player must also be able to get behind the ball and defend when the other team is in possession.

DEFENSIVE STANCE

When you are facing an opponent who has the ball, you must take up a position that makes it difficult to pass or shoot. Bend your knees and stay on your toes so that you can react quickly. Standing with one arm raised and one arm lowered, with both hands open, allows you to prevent both a chest and a bounce pass.

PREVENTING PASS RECEPTION

If you are marking a player who is ready to receive the ball, position yourself alongside your opponent so that you can get your arm across to prevent the pass. Your opponent will try to move away from you, so stay on your toes and keep close without obstructing your opponent.

DEFENCE AGAINST A DRIBBLER

STEP 1
Get your body between the ball and the basket and take up the defensive stance, then move with your opponent as they dribble. Don't get too close, as a quick burst of speed or a side-step will beat you. Just try to block your opponent's path, forcing them away from the basket.

STEP 2
Bend your knees and keep your feet flat on the floor, then by shuffling, rather than taking steps, you can quickly react to your opponent's changes of speed and direction.

When your opponent has the ball, you should make it as hard as possible for him to pass it on to a team-mate.

Watch your opponent's chest, not the ball. That way you are less likely to fall for a fake or dummy shot.

STEP 1

Adopt the defensive stance and keep on your toes, so that you can react to your opponent's moves and fakes.

STEP 2

Use your arms and hands to block any attempt at passing or shooting.

Be aggressive and physical, without actually touching your opponent. If you do, a foul will be awarded against you. The secret of great defending is to use your brain as well as your body. If you anticipate your opponent's next move, you will know how to stop it.

TOP TIP
You must be aware of the movement of both the passer and the pass receiver, so keep both of them in your sight.

ON THE COURT: DEFENDING

It is important that basketball players work on their defensive game and here are some drills that can make it fun.

ZIG-ZAG (2 PLAYERS)

Mark out an area of about 3.5 metres (12 ft) wide and about half a court long. An offensive player must dribble the entire length of this line, keeping the ball alive within the marked out area and travelling in a zig-zag pattern. At the same time, a defensive player tracks this dribble, attempting to disrupt his opponent and/or steal the ball.

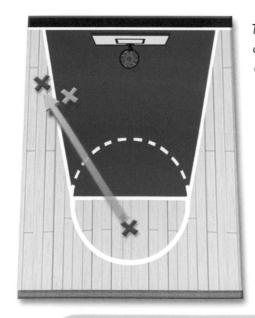

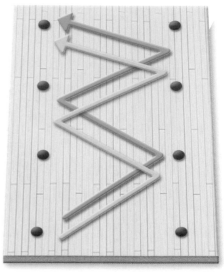

— **Offensive player**
— **Defensive player**

DENIAL DRILL (3 PLAYERS)

This drill requires two offensive players and a defensive player whose role it is to try and prevent pass reception. One offensive player with the ball stands about 5 metres (16 ft) from the other. The defensive player must try to get in front of the pass receiver, moving constantly to make it difficult for the pass to get through.

TOP TIP
If you are defending, try to be roughly two steps in front of your opponent (towards the passer) and only one step away from the line of the intended pass.

TWO-ON-TWO PLAY

Playing two-on-two basketball is a great way to develop all the skills required in the game of basketball – from dribbling and shooting to passing and rebounding. It is a particularly good drill for improving your defending as you are under serious pressure when you or your team-mate do not have the ball.

STEP 1

Two teams of two players play a mini game of basketball in which they both score in the same basket. All players stay within the area of the key. The game is started from the free-throw line and, if one team scores or puts the ball out of play, the other team re-starts.

You must work as a team, making sure that when you are defending you both mark the nearest player and then stick with them until you get a chance to intercept the ball.

STEP 2

When the other team has the ball, you can see what a difference good defensive play makes. If you lose your concentration and your position for a second, you will give the opposition a chance to score.

ADVANCED DRIBBLING

*N*ow you have mastered the basics, it is time to get flash! You should now feel comfortable enough with the basketball in your hands to try the techniques of pro players.

ADVANCE DRIBBLING

If you run in a straight line, dribbling the ball with the same hand, it is easier for a defending opponent to block your path or steal the ball. If you switch hands, or bounce the ball between your legs and behind your back, it gives the opposition little chance to gain possession.

CROSSOVER DRIBBLING

STEP 1
As you dribble forwards, keep your legs apart and your body low. Bring the ball to your side.

STEP 2
Still moving forward, bounce the ball across the front of your body and into your other hand.

STEP 3
Immediately bounce the ball back to the other hand, continuing your forward motion.

STEP 1

As you dribble, step forwards bringing the ball to your side.

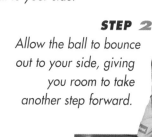

STEP 2

Allow the ball to bounce out to your side, giving you room to take another step forward.

BETWEEN THE LEGS DRIBBLING

STEP 3

Bounce the ball back through your legs – making the gap as wide as you can and guiding the ball cleanly through it – to your other hand again.

This is a tricky skill to perfect, so start off slowly. The temptation is to look down at the ball, but make sure you don't!

STEP 4

Bounce the ball sideways between the gap in your legs, bringing your receiving hand down to collect it.

BEHIND THE BACK DRIBBLING

STEP 1

With your legs wide apart and body position low, bring the ball out to your side.

STEP 2

Looking straight ahead, bounce the ball gently behind you. Bring your other hand behind your back to receive it.

STEP 4

Using the palm of your hand on the top of the ball, ease it back the other way as before.

STEP 3

As the ball touches your receiving hand, bring your arm up with the bounce and out to the side of your body.

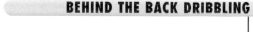

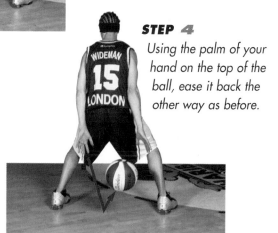

FAKE & DRIVE

*T*he basic skills of basketball allow you to play the game, but if you can master the advanced skills you will turn yourself from a player into a match-winner. The fake and drive is a useful skill to master for real attacking play.

FAKE & DRIVE

The fake and drive is a tactic that is used to confuse your opponent and give yourself space to drive for the basket.

STEP 1
As your path is blocked by a defender, you must quickly look around to find a route to the basket.

STEP 2
Take a fake step to one side, as if you are about to start dribbling forwards. The defender will try to block you.

TOP TIP
Make sure that you don't push your marker aside as you drive forward, as this will result in a foul against you.

STEP 3

As your opponent moves, stop and quickly move back the other way, keeping the ball in the hand farthest away. This will catch your opponent by surprise.

STEP 4

Take a big first step to dribble past your opponent and drive towards the basket. Your opponent will still be struggling to re-adjust.

STEP 5

The successful fake has given you the vital split-second to escape your marker. Now drive straight for the basket, keeping your head up as you look for a chance to shoot or pass.

TIP OFF

A basketball game is started and re-started (after each quarter and some fouls) with a jump ball. Win the ball and put your team in the driving seat.

JUMP BALL

The referee throws the ball up between two players in the centre circle. They must jump up and try to tip it to their team-mates. The two players must not touch the ball until it reaches its highest point, and can only touch it twice. After that it must only be touched by another player.

STEP 1

Crouch opposite your opponent, with your body weight over your toes so that you can easily spring up to the ball when it comes into play.

STEP 2

As the ball is played into the air, time your jump so that you meet the ball at its highest point. Watch the ball as you jump, extending your body and your arms so that you are at full stretch when it starts to come down. If you make it to the ball first, try to tip it to your team-mates who are waiting around the edge of the centre circle.

Be careful not to jump too soon. If you do, you will be on the way back down at the point where you should be at the top of your jump and you will miss the ball!

ADVANCED SHOOTING

If you pull off a hook shot or a slam dunk, not only will your team be two points up but you'll be king of the court!

When the direct route to the basket is blocked, the hook shot can be the only way to get in a shot on the basket.

STEP 1

Move away from your marker by pivoting. Keep your back turned on your opponent to protect the ball.

STEP 2

As you turn, transfer the ball to your shooting hand and cup it with your outstretched fingers. Extend your arm straight out behind you as you lift your back leg off the ground.

STEP 3

As you spring off your forward leg, keep your arm straight and the ball cupped in your shooting hand. Bowl the ball over your head towards the hoop. Release the ball at full stretch and at the top of your jump.

The slam dunk is the most famous shot in basketball because it is the most spectacular. However, you must either be very tall or a superb jumper to pull it off.

STEP 1

Approach the basket running as fast as you can, springing off on your left leg if you have the ball in your right hand (and vice versa).

STEP 2

You need to jump high enough to get the whole ball over the height of the hoop.

STEP 3

If you have gone high enough, you will literally be able to slam the ball down into the basket.

FAST-BREAK DRILLS

Often the best way to score points in basketball is by winning possession during an opposition attack and breaking away while the other team are trying to get back in position. These two drills are designed to ensure that you can fully exploit these situations in a match.

TWO-ON-ONE DRILL (3 PLAYERS)

STEP 1

Two offensive players (A and B) stand on the base-line, one on each of the points where the key line meets the base-line, and a defensive player (C) stands on the base-line under the basket. On the coach's instruction, A and B move the ball up to the halfway line as fast as they can, passing the ball between themselves as they go.

STEP 2

When A and B reach the halfway line, they continue towards the basket. At that point, player C moves forward to the top of the key to defend.

STEP 3

Players A and B must attack the basket under match circumstances – passing, dribbling and shooting their way to a scoring situation as quickly as possible. As soon as they have scored or player C has won the ball, repeat the drill.

STEP 1

Using a full court, three offensive players line up on the base-line, while two defensive players line up on the edge of the key at the opposite end.

STEP 2

On the coach's instruction, the three offensive players move the ball upfield as quickly as they can, creating a three-on-two situation around the opposite basket.

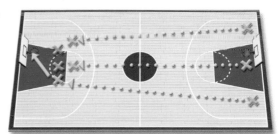

STEP 3

The attacking players must try to engineer a scoring situation.

STEP 4

As soon as a basket is scored, the scoring offensive player joins the previously defensive pair to create a three-on-two attacking situation at the other end.

STEP 5

The two remaining offensive players become the two defenders and must get back to defend the basket at the other end.

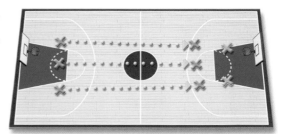

TOP TIP

With both of these drills speed is the key. It may be a practice drill, but try to inject the kind of pace of a real match situation.

FOULS

*I*n theory basketball is a non-contact sport, but with ten players moving at speed in such a tight area inevitably some body contact will occur. However, when players seriously impede their opponents – either intentionally or unintentionally – a personal foul is called.

PERSONAL FOULS

BLOCKING

Any kind of contact which impedes the progress of an opponent.

CHARGING

When a player, with or without the ball, pushes or moves into an opponent.

HAND CHECKING

The use of the hands by a defending player on an opponent, either to impede his progress or assist in his guarding of that opponent.

GUARDING FROM THE REAR

Contact from the rear by a defensive player. The guarding player without the ball is always held responsible for such contact.

HOLDING

Personal contact with an opponent – on any part of his or her body – which interferes with his or her freedom of movement.

ILLEGAL SCREENING

Any attempt to illegally delay or prevent an opponent who does not have control of the ball from reaching their desired position on the court.

PUSHING

Contact when a player forcibly moves or attempts to move an opponent, whether or not he has control of the ball.

ILLEGAL USE OF HANDS

When a player makes contact with an opponent with his hand(s) whilst attempting to play the ball.

DOUBLE FOULS

A double foul is a situation in which two opposing players commit fouls against each other at the same time. When this happens, a personal foul is called against each of the players, but no free throws are awarded. Instead play is re-started by a jump ball at the nearest circle to the two players involved.

WARMING UP & STRETCHING

*W*arming up and stretching before a training session or a match is very important. It reduces the risk of injury and increases a player's speed and ability to twist and turn.

WARMING UP

Before you pick up a ball or even begin stretching it is important to warm up your body. This dramatically lessens your chance of pulling a muscle or a tendon. All you need to do is a light jog for five minutes. This will increase your heart rate and get the blood pumping around your body.

STRETCHING

You must be very careful with your stretching.

– *Never stretch until the body is warmed up.*

– *Always stretch slowly and gently and never so much that it is uncomfortable.*

– *Hold each stretch for 10 to 20 seconds, keeping your body steady at all times.*

– *Never rock or bounce on a stretch.*

– *Breathe out as you stretch.*

– *Stretch both before and after exercise.*

There are hundred of stretches that you can do, but here are some of the most important. Ask a coach or a physiotherapist to show you others and to check that you are doing these right!

GROIN STRETCH

Stand with your legs apart. Then, placing one hand on your thigh, dip your shoulder and lean to one side until you feel slight tension in your groin muscles on that side. Hold the stretch there, then repeat on the other side.

HAMSTRING STRETCH

Lie on your back, and gently lift one leg up in the air. Use your hands to keep the leg straight until you feel tension in your hamstrings at the back of your leg. Hold the stretch there, then repeat with the other leg.

TWO'S COMPANY

Some stretches can be done with a team-mate to keep the stretch steady and straight.

TOUCH YOUR TOES

Gently bend down as if you were going to touch your toes, but stop when you feel tension in the back of your legs. Hold the stretch for 10 seconds and then try reaching down a little more. Slowly you should be able to reach further and further until you can actually get right down.

CALF STRETCH

Put the weight of your body on the front foot, bending the knee and stretching the other leg behind with your heel up. Then lean forward so that your hands touch the ground and slowly push your outstretched leg back.

PRACTICE SHOTS

Warming up your body before a match is most important. But it is also important to practice shooting hoops, to get your brain into gear and your hand-eye co-ordination up to speed.

DIET & MENTAL ATTITUDE

It is not possible to make yourself a more skillful player by eating certain foods, but you can give yourself more energy and stamina on the pitch by eating and drinking the right foods. This food chart gives you the basic principles of a balanced diet, ideal for athletes.

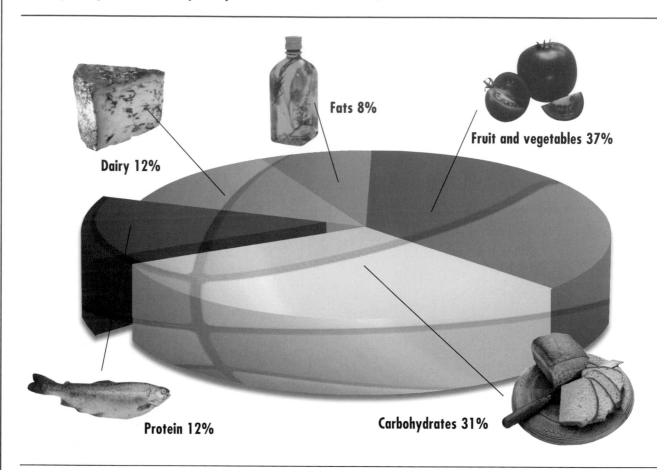

Dairy 12%

Fats 8%

Fruit and vegetables 37%

Protein 12%

Carbohydrates 31%

ENERGY BUSTERS

If you are doing a lot of exercise, then you need to cut down on fatty foods and eat plenty of carbohydrates to provide the energy for all the exercise that you are doing.

You do need protein (required for the growth and repair of the body after exercise), but try to choose low-fat sources, such as fish or chicken.

BEFORE THE MATCH

Basketball is a non-stop, end-to-end game, which means that you need to eat a high-carbohydrate meal at least three hours before playing to provide enough energy to see you through the game.

Low-fat pasta or rice dishes (without creamy sauce) are ideal. Then, in the run-up to the game, boost your carbohydrate level with fast-digesting snacks such as bananas or dried fruit. It is also crucial to drink plenty of liquid before a game and throughout it. Water or isotonic sports drinks consumed two or three hours before playing will make up for the water you will lose (through sweat) during the game.

MENTAL ATTITUDE

As well as preparing the body, it is also important to prepare the mind for a basketball match.
In all sports, much of your ability as a player comes from self-confidence and self-belief. If you believe that you are going to win the match or that you are going to score that free-throw, chances are you will.

MENTAL PREPARATION

More and more sports coaches are using methods of coaching that focus on the psychological side as well as the physical. Pro basketball clubs will often use a sports psychologist to work with the players on their positive thinking and concentration, as well as building up faith in themselves and their team-mates.

Basketball is such a quick game that it is essential not to lose concentration for a moment – during that moment you might lose your opponent or fumble the ball. Try to focus all the time, never letting your mind drift from the game for even a second. Some teams also like to focus together, gathering into a huddle before the match or at the end of a time-out. Basketball is a team game, and it is important that the team is together. If you are, and you believe in each other, you will be more prepared to run yourself through the pain barrier for your team-mates and they will be prepared to do the same.

HOW THE FAMOUS DO IT

Most people just play basketball for fun, but imagine if you got to play every day and got paid for it. It's a great life for players in the NBA or the top European leagues, but don't think it is all glamour and glory in the pro game – it takes hard work and dedication to make it and stay at the top.

LIFE IN THE NBA

The peak of world basketball is the NBA in America. It features the best teams and arenas in the world – and the best players.

But it is not all bright lights and slam dunking for these stars. An NBA player has to work hard. Each team plays 82 games every season (more if they reach the play-offs), and with away games all over the States that means some serious time on the road. To play this often at such a high level, players must be incredibly fit – like the high scoring Minnesota Timberwolves player, Kevin Garnett. Even during the closed season, players are expected to work on their fitness and many will go back to their old college teams to keep up their match practice.

TYPICAL NBA MATCH DAY (HOME)

9:00 Wake up.

9:30 Eat breakfast.

10:00 Drive to practice.

11:00 Team practice, including stretching, jogging, shooting and rebounding practice. Work on new plays, some sprints and finish with endless free throws.

12:00 Watch videos of recent games and tonight's opponents.

1:00 Drive back home to rest.

2:00 Eat a carbohydrate-laden lunch and drink plenty of liquid.

5:00 Return to the arena and get changed.

6:00 Go out on court to warm up and take practice shots.

7:00 Head back into locker room where the coach will go over last-minute tactics.

7:40 Showtime. The introduction to an NBA game resembles a star-studded Hollywood movie premiere. The lights dim, music blares and a multi-media laser light show all lead to the introduction of the starting five players from each team.

8:00 Four quarters of non-stop NBA action.

11:00 Media interviews. Win or lose, players are required to speak to the media after the game.

12:00 Shower and eat a team meal.

12:30 Go home, or board a team bus. Tomorrow could bring another match in another city.

MEDIA WORK

If you are a top basketball player in the NBA, everyone wants to know your opinion of the game.

There are hundreds of TV and radio shows, newspapers,z magazines and internet websites dedicated to basketball. Part of a player's job is to answer questions and pose for photographs. TV companies pay vast sums to show pro basketball games, and as part of the deal cameras will often be allowed access to the pitch side and dressing-room areas where players and coaches are contractually obliged to give interviews.

MONEY

Top basketball players, such as Shaquille O'Neal of the Miami Heat (*right*), earn millions of dollars every season. In addition to their basketball earnings, they also endorse products (like sportswear or trainers).

However, those playing in less high-profile leagues in Europe and around the world are not so wealthy.

RULES

There are hundreds of rules and sub-rules in basketball but we don't have room for them all here. These are the basics, and they are always enforced by the referee.

TIMING

Under international rules a basketball match is divided into four quarters of 10 minutes (in the NBA they have four quarters of 12 minutes each). However, the clock is stopped frequently during a match, and in real-time most games last about 90 minutes. If the scores are level at full-time, the teams play five minutes of overtime (and then another five until there is a winner) – there are no drawn matches in basketball.

TIME-OUTS

Coaches are allowed to stop the play once in each quarter and twice in the last quarter – for a maximum of one minute – to discuss tactics with their players. In overtime, they are allowed only one time-out.

24-SECOND RULE

In the NBA when a team gains possession of the ball, they have 24 seconds in which to shoot. If they fail to do so, they lose possession.

8-SECOND RULE

After gaining possession inside their own half, the attacking team must move the ball into the opposition's half within 8 seconds. Again, if they fail to do so they lose possession.

5-SECOND RULE

A player must take a throw-in or a free-throw within 5 seconds (in the NBA, players have 10 seconds to take a free throw).

3-SECOND RULE

Players are only allowed to be in their opposition's restricted area (the key) for 3 seconds at a time – they must leave before 3 seconds.

CLOSELY-GUARDED PLAYER

If a player is closely marked he must either pass, dribble or shoot within five seconds of receiving the ball or possession is awarded to the opposition. This rule does not exist in the NBA.

FREE THROW

A free throw is an unchallenged shot at the basket, taken from behind the free-throw line on the edge of the key. All players, other than the shooter, must stand outside the key in the designated free-throw lanes (or behind the thrower, outside the three point line). Free throws are awarded for various fouls and a basket scores one point.

PERSONAL FOUL

This is an infringement of the rules involving body contact with an opponent (see pages 38–39). Such fouls are punished with a throw-in to the opposition or, if the fouled player was in the process of shooting, one or more free-throws to be taken by the fouled player (for instance, three free-throws if the shot was being attempted from outside the three point line).

TECHNICAL FOUL

This is an infringement of the rules involving bad behaviour, such as arguing with opponents or officials. These fouls are punished with two free throws (taken by a player designated by the captain).

DISQUALIFYING FOUL

This is a serious foul on an opponent, such as a punch, punished by instant dismissal from the game.

FIVE-FOUL RULE

When a player has committed five fouls (either personal or technical), he is dismissed from the game and may not return. In the NBA, the rule is six fouls.

VIOLATION

A foul awarded for a violation of the rules, such as an illegal dribble or spending more than three seconds in the restricted area. A violation is punished by awarding the ball to the opposition, usually with a throw-in.

GOAL TENDING

Players must not touch the ball when it is on its downward flight towards the basket, and defenders are not allowed to touch the ball when it is in the basket (otherwise they would be able to push the ball back out through the hoop!). If this violation is committed by the offensive team, no point can be scored and the ball is awarded to the opposition at the free-throw line. If it is committed by the defence, the shooter is awarded the appropriate points, as if the ball had gone through the basket.

OUT OF BOUNDS

A player is out of bounds if they touch or cross any boundary line taking it out of court. The ball is out of bounds when the player in possession goes out of bounds, or the ball itself touches or crosses a boundary line. However, the ball cannot be out of bounds until it touches the floor. When this happens, the throw-in goes against the team who last touched the ball.

BALL RETURNED TO BACK COURT

When a team has moved the ball from inside their own half into their opposition's half, they are not allowed to move back over the halfway line otherwise the ball goes to the other team.

GLOSSARY

ASSIST – A pass that leads to a team-mate scoring.

BASKET – The hoop and net through which the ball must go to record a score. Also the name for a score.

BACKBOARD – The rectangle behind the basket off which the ball is allowed to rebound.

BACK COURT – The half of the court which a team defends.

BOXING OUT– The positioning of a player between the basket and an opponent to win a rebound.

BOUNCE PASS – A pass where the ball is bounced off the ground to a team-mate.

CHEST PASS – A short, direct pass made at chest height.

COURT – The playing area for a basketball match.

DEFENCE – When a team has the ball, the other team is on defence to try and stop them scoring.

DRIBBLING – Moving around the court whilst dribbling the ball..

DRIVE – An aggressive dribble directly towards the basket.

FAKE – When a player pretends to move or throw the ball one way, but stops an goes the other to fool an opponent.

FIELD GOAL – A my basket scored, with the exception of free throws, from anywhere on the three point line.

FOUL – An illegal play.

Free throw – An unopposed shot, taken from behind the free throw line and awarded after an opposing foul.

FRONT COURT – The half of the court a team is attacking.

HOOK SHOT – A shot where the ball is played over a players' head from alongside the basket.

HOOP – The circular section of the basket which the ball must go through to score.

JUMP BALL – Used to start and re-start the game, with two opposing players jumping against each other to win a ball thrown by the referee.

JUMP SHOT – A shot played while the shooter is jumping in the air.

KEY – The restricted area underneath the basket at each end.

LAY-UP-SHOT – When you take one and a half steps to towards the net.

NBA – National Basketball Association.

OFFENCE – When a team is in possession of the ball, they are on offence and trying to score.

OVERHEAD PASS – A pass to a team-mate played above the head.

OVERTIME – An extra period of five minutes played if the scores are level at full-time.

PIVOTING – Turning on the spot while holding the ball.

REBOUND – A shot that misses the basket and bounces back off the hoop or backboard.

REFEREE – The official in charge of a basketball match. At the top level there may be more than one referee in a match.

SET SHOT – A straight shot at the basket, taken with both feet on the ground.

SLAM DUNK – A shot where the ball is held above the basket and then forced downwards through it.

STEAL – Legally gaining possession of the ball from a dribbler or passer.

THREE-POINTER – See 'Field goal'.

THROW-IN – A free throw from the side-line.

TIME-OUT – A one-minute break in play called by the coach.

TIP IN – A shot where the ball is rebounded off the backboard into the basket.

TRIPLE THREAT POSITION – The standard position to protect the ball, adopted when players receive the ball.